Emma's First Day of Kindergarten

by Suzan Johnson
Illustrated by Rudra Bose

This book is dedicated to Wendy T.
who always encouraged me
and shared my books with her students.
You will be missed.

Emma was going to start kindergarten tomorrow. She was attending school with her brother Ethan.

Ethan and Emma packed their book bags as they talked excitedly about the first day.

"I cannot wait to see all of my friends," her brother said.

Emma wasn't so sure about starting her first day of kindergarten.

As she fell asleep that night, she had an uneasy feeling in her tummy.

On the morning of the first day of school, there was a buzz in the house.

Everyone chattered with smiles.

Everyone except Emma.

She played with her breakfast, instead.

As Emma, her brother, and dad approached the front of the school, they noticed Emma's teacher standing outside and waving everyone in.

Ethan swam into the building and waved goodbye with a huge smile on his face.

Emma stood outside of the school and held on tight to her dad's hand. Emma's dad reminded her that they had met her teacher Mrs. Seashell last week.

He said, "Mom is going to pick you up right after school."

Emma smiled a wobbly grimace and said, "see you later" as she swam toward the front door.

Emma's father stood outside and waved until Emma vanished inside of the school doors.

Emma nervously sat at the table with her name on it.

As Emma looked around the classroom, some of the other students were talking and laughing. Some others sat and looked anxious like Emma.

Then, she remembered what her papa said and put a smile on her face.

Mrs. Seashell swam to the front of the room and told them all about herself and what they were going to do next. Emma liked Mrs. Seashell and began to relax until it was time for the kinder mermaids to share something about themselves.

As Melinda, the little girl who was next to Emma, talked about her pet seahorse, Emma began to sweat.

When it was Emma's turn, she froze. Emma felt as if she could not move.

The other students smiled, and it seemed to encourage her. Emma said she was glad to be in the class. She then talked about her family and all of her favorite things.

After sharing time, Mrs. Seashell gave everyone a paper and asked all of the kinder mermaids to write their names five times on the paper for practice.

Emma was happy because she was good at it.

The rest of the school day flew by!

There was so much to do in school, and Emma loved it all!

She only realized it was time to go home when the bell rang.

Emma's mom was waiting for her right outside of the front door.

As Emma swam to her mom, she thought about everything she was going to tell her about her first day of school.

Emma was ready to go back tomorrow! She wanted to find out what she would do next in kindergarten.

Words To Know

<u>Froze</u>: to become physically firm or solid.

<u>Grimace</u>: to distort one's face in an expression usually of pain, disgust, or disapproval.

<u>Mermaid</u>: a fabled marine creature with the head and upper body of a human and the tail of a fish.

<u>Seahorse</u>: a small fish with bony plates covering its body and a head that looks like a horse's head.

*Merriam-Webster Dictionary

Acrostic Poem

M
E
R
M
A
I
D

Other Books by Suzan Johnson

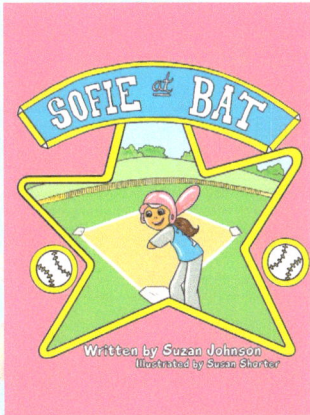

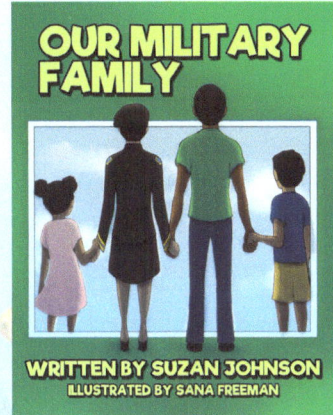

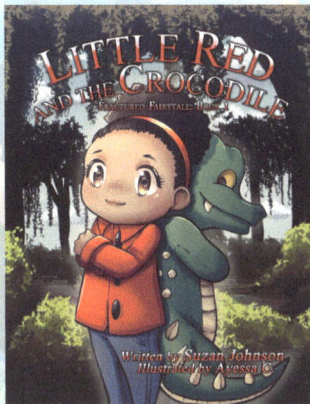

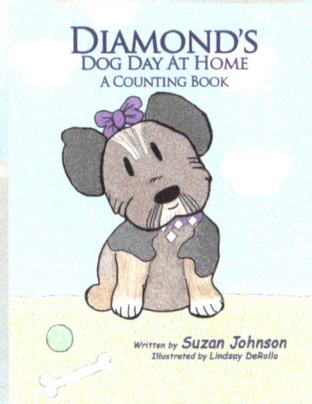

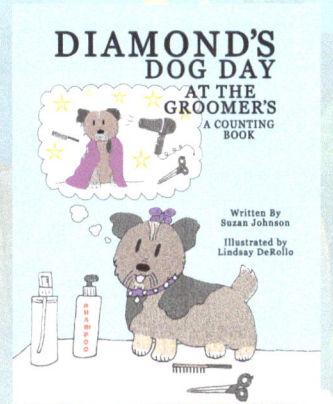

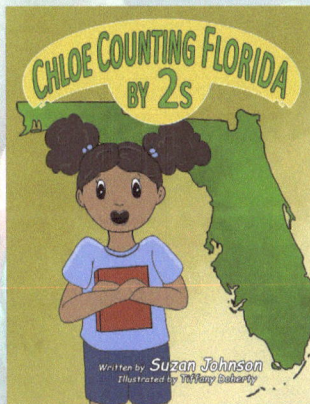

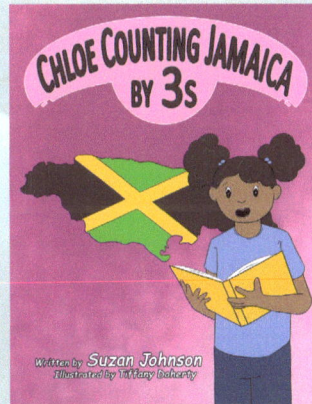

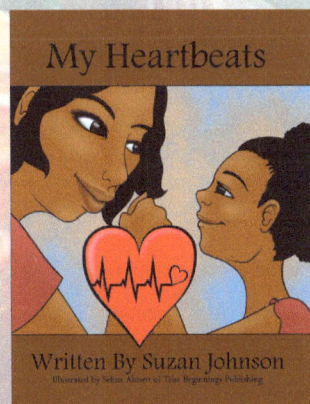

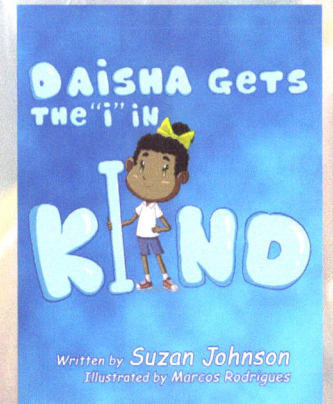

SOFIE at BAT
Written by Suzan Johnson
Illustrated by Susan Shorter

SOFIE at DANCE
Written by Suzan Johnson
Illustrated by Susan Shorter

OUR MILITARY FAMILY
WRITTEN BY SUZAN JOHNSON
ILLUSTRATED BY SANA FREEMAN

LITTLE RED AND THE CROCODILE
A Blended Fairytale
Written by Suzan Johnson
Illustrated by Ayesslo

DIAMOND'S DOG DAY AT HOME
A COUNTING BOOK
Written by Suzan Johnson
Illustrated by Lindsay DeRollo

DIAMOND'S DOG DAY AT THE GROOMER'S
A COUNTING BOOK
Written By Suzan Johnson
Illustrated by Lindsay DeRollo

CHLOE COUNTING FLORIDA BY 2s
Written by Suzan Johnson
Illustrated by Tiffany Doherty

CHLOE COUNTING JAMAICA BY 3s
Written by Suzan Johnson
Illustrated by Tiffany Doherty

CHLOE COUNTING NEW YORK BY 5s
Written by Suzan Johnson
Illustrated by Tiffany Doherty

My Heartbeats
Written By Suzan Johnson
Illustrated by Seise Abner et. Tao Beginnings Publishing

CHLOE COUNTING WORKBOOK
Written by Suzan Johnson
Illustrated by Tiffany Doherty

DAISHA GETS THE "i" IN KIND
Written by Suzan Johnson
Illustrated by Marcos Rodrigues

Other Books by Suzan Johnson

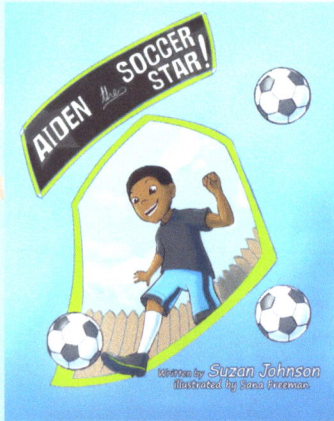

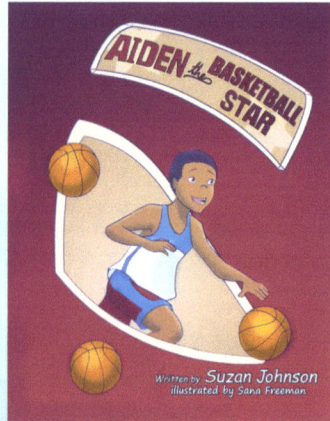

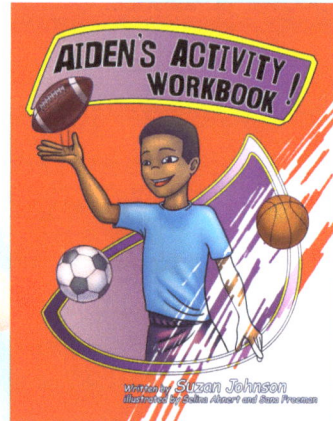

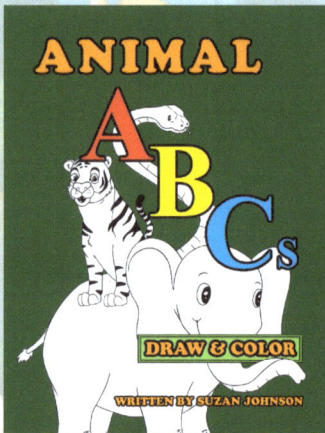

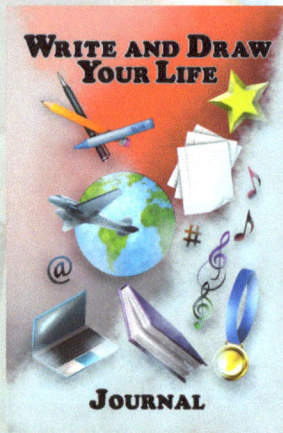

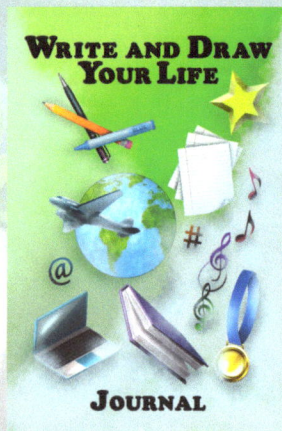

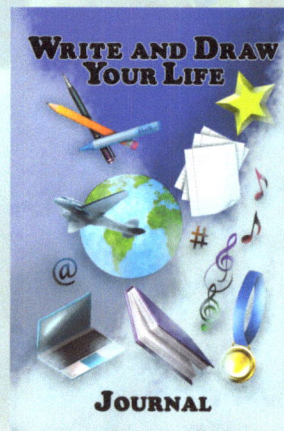

www.ingramcontent.com/pod-product-compliance
Lightning Source LLC
LaVergne TN
LVHW072059070426

835508LV00002B/167